THE BLOND TEXTS
&
THE AGE OF EMBERS

by Nadia Tuéni
Translated by Amir Parsa

 UpSet Press, Inc.
P.O. Box 200340
Brooklyn, NY 11220
www.upsetpress.org

English translations © by Amir Parsa 2012
Original text (*Les textes blonds* & *L'âge d'écume*) copyrighted by Fondation Nadia Tuéni
and Editions Dar An-Nahar
Published by arrangement with Dar An-Nahar Publishing.
Dar An-Nahar Publishing is the sole owner of copyright to all Nadia Tuéni's books.

Cover artwork by Golnaz Fathi
Cover and text design by Aaron Kenedi

UPSET PRESS is an independent press based in Brooklyn. The original impetus of the press was to upset the status quo through literature. The press has expanded its mission to promote new work by new authors; the first works, or complete works, of established authors, including restoring to print new editions of important texts; and first time translations of works into English. Overall, the Press endeavors to advance authors' innovative visions and bodies of work that engender new directions in literature.

Established in 2000, UpSet Press organized readings and ran writing workshops until 2005, when it published its first book, *Theater of War*, by Nicholas Powers. The Press has increased its publishing efforts in recent years and has multiple titles forthcoming in 2013. The University of Arkansas Press became the official distributor of UpSet Press in 2011. For more information, visit upsetpress.org.

Library of Congress Control Number: 2012951034

First printing, November 2012
ISBN 9780976014294
Printed in the USA
10 9 8 7 6 5 4 3 2 1

CONTENTS

PUBLISHER'S NOTE

I first read Nadia Tuéni several years ago when I came across a selection of her poems, *Lebanon: Poems of Love and War*, translated by Samuel John Hazo and Paul B. Kelley, published by Syracuse University Press. I quickly sought out more of her poetry and, just as quickly, was frustrated to learn that the majority of her poetry had not been translated into English. Her body of work included several prominent literary accolades but nowhere could I find an English translation aside from the above book, and even that was a sparse selection of poems from her last two books. There were six or seven other poetry collections that stared at me in French, untranslated, beseeching. And so I began a prolonged effort to acquire the permissions necessary to translate the early work of Nadia Tuéni.

I'm exceedingly grateful to Dar An-Nahar and the Tuéni family for the opportunity and trust granted UpSet Press to translate such an innovative poet. In particular, I would like to thank Nayla Tuéni, Jana Tamer and Samia Shami for their insight and assistance throughout the completion of this project. I'm equally grateful to Amir Parsa for his dedication, approach, and the integrity with which he performed these translations. Also, I'd like to thank Golnaz Fathi for providing the cover art (magnificent and fitting), Matthew Rotando for his editorial assistance, and the SYMA organization for their generous support to help fund the publication of this book.

UpSet Press is proud to introduce Nadia Tuéni to a new readership in English. Ultimately, I hope this translation is just the beginning of a larger endeavor to translate the complete poems of Nadia Tuéni.

—ROBERT BOORAS
Brooklyn, 2012

TRANSLATOR'S NOTE

In the train the subway the métro; in the park on the bench at the tables of the coffee shops—and cafés; by the side of a dying woman; hanging unto a strap on the bus in the middle of rush hour; on the platforms, in the apart', at the long table at the lounge by the New York home, at Zéglo's in Paris, in another park, Brooklyn, Manhattan, Queens; on the airplane and in the cars, and more places still: with Nadia... Nadia's texts, rather, Nadia's voice(s), Nadia's words, stanzas and... unusual punctuation—and lack thereof! (And I'm a champion of unusual punctuation practice!) Her images, her rhymes, her rhythms. Her thoughts, her cries, her anguish and her, yes, silences. Translation... How long I have thought of the inappropriateness of the term. And the madness to engage (or, agree to engage), especially when it comes to poetry, of course. And yet, here again, somehow... Theory and practice crucial as always: with translation seen as a writing practice too—and the translatory oeuvre as a performance, a work within the body of work of the poet/writer. With: stylistic adherences and shifts, formal reflections, cultural agency: more to come on all this, I promise (or rather: hope), soon, much more, but now, through Nadia, with Nadia: a world—hers: re-writing in, what, English, American, American English?

Nadia Tuéni's texts are infused with an authentic passion and an overall rawness that speak to her existential and poetic encounter with the world. A unique worldview and linguistic twists that fashion images at once jarring, playful, disconcerting and surprising. Her first two books: and thus, one finds some awkwardness—and unique choices, but the overall effect is powerful and memorable. (Still, the temptations: to add, delete, edit, re-write too... But no: even the translator-writer, the writer-translator, does not into those realms tread! So: hold steady, hold back, bring forth even those characteristics and attributes: among the fabulous pieces, the awkward ones: those too, let them be. Sure, the translator is a re-creator, but a certain type of re-creator...) Powerful—and impactful in a singular way: Nadia's was a dissenting voice at once fond of her country's natural and mythical landscapes, yet critical of habits, conventions, and rituals. Through powerful tropes and surrealistic juxtapositions of images (and sentences, and strophes, that at times have seemingly little to do with one another), her poems challenge us in unexpected manners, inviting the imagined readers into a labyrinthine otherworld while remaining full of mystery and ambiguity. At times difficult to decipher, at others surprisingly accessible through the introduction of fairy-tale characters and child-like phrases: short yet powerful texts constantly redirecting the reader and imparting a potent mix of anguish and wonderment akin to one's lived experience. The personal suffering that she endured after the death of her young daughter is everywhere present in these volumes, a personal tragedy that she molds into a heartfelt work, constructing ultimately a portrait and an experience of unimaginable loss.

Throughout her writing career, Tuéni remained independent and unattached to fashionable schools of thought. Her fondness for her native land is intertwined with her need to reflect upon the realities and conditions that surrounded her. The operations at work in her poetry—from the varied linguistic play to the jarring juxtapositions, from the ambiguity of certain passages to the playful manipulations of syntax—are intensely original and delightfully strange. Scenes from her own childhood accompany imagery drawn from Christian mythology and rituals, while tales of lovers scorned are juxtaposed with those of gods abandoned. Revelatory descriptions of springs, mountains and street-scenes accompany metaphysical contemplations, themselves masked by layers of striking imagery. Forceful and meditative, two books that present internal and emotional landscapes as well as a sensual if fragmented portrait of her urban and natural surroundings. The present translation of Tuéni's work will allow for a striking strand of Lebanese Francophone literature to be presented to a wider English-speaking audience. It should, in addition, initiate extensive conversations around literary and cultural traditions of a region that is in our day too easily morphed into a homogeneous caricature. As always, exploring literature from the peripheries of a language (here, French) leads to the discovery of extraordinary work done by writers living at these margins and in these intersecting spaces.

—AMIR PARSA

THE BLOND TEXTS

PROLOGUE

Braided with stars
threaded sky
the country I go to.
Gray cathedral
stage lights
to renounce.
Wandering hands
other sunsets
have discovered
this continent.
Nothing is weaned
everything is transmitted
in the country I go to.
Neglected bruises
Sanskrit terms
and night flights
to exhaust
this long journey!

THE COUNTRY I GO TO

For a little girl
who loved fairy tales

On the cypress hill
two wise goblins met.
– What are you doing around here?
– Well just like you, I've come to visit the enchanted green country.
The little girl announced their arrival
braiding a wreath of songs
with her blond hair.
Then she put her little hands
in their little goblin paws:
– Leave your wisdom here
you must not bore
the characters of a fairy tale.
It's Noddy the dwarf
it's Merlin the wizard
who in the evening visit the moon
up there on its perch.
Here come the fairy dames and Puss 'n Boots
and adorned flowers for the masquerade
of the enchanted glade.
Good evening blue bird and my Snow White
hello gray dove and the entire cortege
from Prince Charming to Sleeping Beauty.
My friend the river gurgles as it steers
the coming of spring
and right next door the sorcerer's tree
plucks the days of a calendar…

But here Time has gotten so comfortable
it has stopped
and our two goblins are aghast
to see exist
all that they ignored!
The little girl has taken them back to the silver doors!
– Come back and see us one day if you find
the way to the enchanted world!

On the cypress hill
two wise goblins met.
– What are you doing around here?
– Well just like you I've come to search for
the fingers of the fairy tale!

Once upon at time
    there was me
    and also you
once upon a time
    there was them
    both of them
but they took her from me
if only I knew who
    and why
once she was gone
my life splintered in two
then everything resumed
but not like before.
Once upon a time
    there was me
    and also you
once upon a time
    there was them
    not both of them!

On the other side of the mirror
I turned the page
and saw the illusion boasting.
The stone is vibrant.
Ancient maps and their ornate outlines
flatter the present.
At the heart of desire I put the hearth
and on the dust of its lost continents
through the whirlwinds of sand
jackals prowl.
The hand of an innocent child
shatters the mirror with a simple flip
and the footsteps of millions of years
collide
there in the mirror!

In a small dish the stew of a bird
rebelling against eternity burns
and the green temples of vegetable gods
mark the path on evening bridges.

I went back there.

On the other side of the mirror
a life that is not mine gets erased
and the splendor of creation sculpts her face.

Obsession moves towards its origin
where the mage perishes.
The torrent digs its bed of deception
around the log
but all has not been said
and defiant I went back
there in my mirror!

I saw the palettes
in colors of blood
and amulets outside time
give their toll to the night stars.
The twisted rope of all sighs
and the layers of all desires tighten.

I will find the sand again
the engulfed mage and the royal bird,
the drawing etched on the wind's stone,
my candles and their extinguishers
that were reflected
there in my mirror!

Prisoner of the word he escaped
the citadels in the sky pointed at him
and his banners and his palfreys
all tainted in gold
preceded me
at the edge of dawns.
It's in a little while
and not yesterday anymore
that Ophelia nurses
her childlike gestures!

In a freewheeling dance
a little girl fled
frail and florid
towards infinite and
sinister countries
for endless time
without return.
And yet one day I found her
a floating elf in the pine forest
her blue soul reflected
in her deep liquid eyes,
heavy secrets of another world
dissolved in her white and pale
while her blond hair braided rays of light
under the pines.
Dream of a sun ready to disappear
a gust of wind was already carrying her
adorned with regrets of a forgotten world.
Then she smiled and told me:
Green are these countries.
Then she left
and then it's over.

You don't resemble anything
and I don't have the words to tell them about you.
What I found there was so different
I have almost forgotten it.

There are other countries in other Milky Ways
where other rainbows full of sorrows
make life explode with intense pleasure.
Where hell is inhabited by a tender and gentle soul
where the harmony of places allows one to await
always, in an instant, what needs to be accomplished.
I am a child in these countries and time is no longer my master
space envelops me and yet it is I
who owns it with an embrace and slowly crushes it.
This is where the ultimate gestation turns
your absurdity into clarity, your nothingness into fiction.
For a long time I cried for you from these faraway countries
in the pine forest and you ignored me.
You didn't hear, you didn't want to understand
this silent song these spirals of joy
this hymn to something other
this cult of other laws.
And yet one day I thought you were smiling at me
it was when bent over a white tile,
silent shadow mask of a punished child,
from the depths of your color
I had a premonition of infinity!

On a livid face
an ardent thrust
and moving halos
carry away inertia.
I scattered my being
in the winds of your seasons
the broken bells
forced me to appear
stripped of illusions
and the silk ladder
that leads to the other side
mutated into a cordage.
Savagely anchored
I lost the route
to the isles of destiny
for a familiar sound
I refused the key
to my imagination.

To know is to haunt
when to leave is to be born,
born to difference, to other designs—
and the stem of a rose is no less
the substance of the rose!

Opaline vision
I recognized you for having hardened you!

When I met you
on the tender planet
the air had the stench of dullness
you smiled at me
and on your cold lips
I thought I would die of boredom

When I possessed you
on the arid planet
the wind was sweeping my loves
and I felt
with you in my arms
nothing but great disgust

When I found you again
on the strange planet
it was indeed you I was searching for
to quench
in the layers of your soul
my thirst for ambiguity

And when I lost you
on the obscure planet
I thought I would die from it
but I was promised
that you would return in my future
and I lived because of it!

I collected hatred
and I wallowed in it
I cultivated it
I distilled it
I asked you to share it
but I saw fear in your cowardly eyes.
You see, Narcissus
if it's not given to everyone
to know how to love
to hate beautifully
is a gourmet's prerogative.
One must like an esthete
know how to appreciate
this great gamble
and take one's time.
Believe me it's not
for ordinary folk!

Under an old olive tree the jasmine bursts open
and my youth flows
scents of sweet basil and flowers of dry thyme
and cicadas in the velvet pines
sing a hymn to the sun
send gratitude for existing

for the red tiles
on the slopes of valleys
and the sea that sways
and a blue that leaves you breathless

and you the Bedouin
with Arabian eyes
how the Western winds
have changed you!

A lascivious arch
a rusty arabesque
a silent cloister
punctuated by fig trees
my lovers have passed
under a white veil
tanned lovers
for an odalisque
in the span of one summer...

Towards the blue sun
the amaranth flower
the bird that goes silent
and life that sings

Towards a naked soul
towards a body offered
pure in its sin
beautiful in its truth

Towards the red plains
the dried-up spring
the giant's tree

Towards a planet
at the very end of time
towards everything repeated
and everything understood

Towards an adventure
masked as fate
towards a you and a me
towards always tomorrow!

I sifted through my days
and rummaged through my nights
trampled the dream
exhumed forgetting
I lived my dear!

I sold love
cashed in the prize
I sank hatred
buried boredom
I lived my dear!

I took off the mask
and molded the yearning
I chewed on sorrow
and threw away the fruit
I lived my dear!

I shouted amen
then laughed about it
found other themes
tasted madness
I lived my dear!

I gave life
drew pleasure from few
and from many too
savored every last drop
I lived my dear!

But I believed in him
surrendered myself
melted in his bed
drank to his essence
and I died from it my dear!

Under a white gown
the revolution roared
it took everything
the good and the bad.
On virgin land
one must begin anew
and build again
to better destroy afterwards.

On an island of nothingness
a life was grafted
then it overflowed
and the star above
a million years away
glimmering in its glory
flees toward its destiny
as the night of always
is baptized cloudless.

I caressed a shadow
and you followed it
I imagined it
and you saw it take life

Under a deceptive portrait
the image splits in two
and the insolent laughter
rings out like a lost bet

Bet of a presence
here and beyond
beyond myself
and all my ruffles

Beyond the instant
when I sensed her presence
beyond now
beyond a life.

Plural multiple and still
always alone.

At seven at eight and at minus infinity
the period of mourning is punished.
The voodoo of numbers
pierces the uncertain realm
the mystical movements of the steam boat
stir up the shroud
and in the whirlwind
the day appears with its alluvia.
At nine at ten and at minus everything
I threw away the urge
the urge to know where I am.
Check to you and checkmate to life.
I took my queen, liberated my tower
while up there sister Anne in a trance
curses this heavy sun
that plunges out of boredom!
At one at two I know your refrain
to turn always and extend a hand
then the merry-go-round goes farther and farther away—
long live the deaf for hearing nothing!

In a sea of clay, Pandora,
I was submerged
and the birds of prey in steel spirals
were divvying up my soul.
But through them, Pandora, there was you!
I loved you in another time
when through unknown waters
I searched the barges of forgetting you had fashioned,
when the sweet horror of the ocean's abyss
had the sinister reflection of your eyes
I slumped towards you, Pandora,
in this turbulence of green flotsam!
And for a new voice, for a new tone
I gave my soul for the price of a poppy.

You offered me your forbidden visions
and your carbuncles tamed my body
sabbath of red and gold
a path of rocks sprinkled with spoils
and the winds of sand and the blue mirage
for a death by two.
On the slope of desire, a distressed breath
and the residue of forgetting for the flower of my cherry tree.
I gave you the dread of mornings without light,
imprint of a rock on this inclined dream.
The fisherman's credo on a sea of doubts
the next step sketched to the melody of fate.
A cloth woven with venom, and also with innocence,
Cesar's bed encumbered with puppets,
and the figureheads of tomorrow's vessels surge!

A gaze is enough for hatred to germinate
and for anguish to unfurl in the depths of galaxies
a gaze is enough for my being to carry
your wreckage to the summit of pleasure

A gaze is enough for snow to cry
and for love's essence to rise
a gaze is enough to get mangled and run away
and another gaze for the dream to explode

A gaze is enough for the rock to growl
a gaze that embraces and molds the universe
a gaze is enough to see extended in prayer
a life full of vast and soft nothingness!

Two eyes,
one soul
a cry of joy:
a little something and other paths,
the cruelty of origins
and the splendor of ephemera.
Two features
ageless
a paleness
the strange norm of colors,
blues of other worlds to embroil
the white regrets
of an opaline with a weary complexion.
A laughter
a shadow
a wood fire
andirons in the shape of remembrance.
Two loops
a melody
a time for respite
in the swelter
of this summer!

MARINE DIVERSION

The hermit crab is a shellfish
saint shellfish with sumptuous pomp,
for a field of gods he has his beach
and for his obsession the pebbles.
Denounce yourself on an aquamarine reef
you poor thing,
these green moons are nothing but rhymes
and the whirlpools mere playthings.
For the nerite snail the defiance of sex,
for the giant clam the eyes of a madman
and then Venus laments
of not having understood a thing!
Coral reefs
marine lights
a school of piranhas,
to fashion suns
in the abyss
and not explode from it!

I threw my joy over the moon
and she hummed the laughter of time
and faith, swept over the dune,
came back from it on a seagull.
The day wanted to harpoon this ritual,
impose consistency, erode the laws.
The winds said: "Way too early for you!"
Forget the labyrinth and the straight path
it's the byroad that takes one far!
Those who want to believe in me
will have to go far, back to my twenties,
to the point where in the flow of a sad story
I decline my turn to choose
between a masquerade
and this long detour!

To tarnish the brilliance of constellations
you sharpen your teeth
better balancing on their truth
the dust of years!
There is nothing left, nothing left to find
in the pious English garden.
The wait has ended in bridal feasts
of elsewhere and earth,
and on the embankment strewn with steps
the footprints smile one last time.
She conspired with masts
for the wind's embrace.
A cold breath wounds the madman
and comes to bewitch this arid dolmen
where a druid presides on a skiff.
Then for the anguish of sacred gestures
I placed the sound and its driftings.
The race is open, the page is turned
for a warhorse to be ridden by lancers,
I screamed: "Come back and share my digs
strap my body to your stirrups,
and through an error a complaint a doubt
set my sailboat toward the deceptive sun!"

The shadow of the cypress tree to measure my troubles
and its heritage to accept them.
The flip of hands playing like moths
nourishing fire to transcend them!
A grid of stars dresses regret
when the hand of fate
smacks its dark comet!
Why delay the march of winds?
The imprint has pooled the tears of stones
while the lying oracle in prayer
overlaid the sky to fit the conceit of time.
Come back and find me somewhere
I will tell you children's tales
fables lost at the edge of evening
and in an echo, on a promenade,
the gods exhaust themselves with laughter!

In the shelter of a grove of heliotropes
a ladybug bemoans her fate.
The hailstorm washed away
the strophe it had inherited.
The rhyme is destined to unknown ends
the nova borne of a song,
and the holy stanza carved at the foot of the heliotrope
by the ladybug demands a ransom.
The last word of the story will not come back
to illuminate the foil with cursive letters.
Among the asphodels the halos of disgrace
have redrawn the fresco and its ceiling.
Did you check the pile of lies?
All the fables of ladybugs that have been told!
Is it him, is it you, who spread
the heliotropes like pawns in the forest?

DIAGONAL

To the one offering the most
throw the fervor of your twenties,
the steep incline of an escape
on the lichen with the blond text.
Sow the fear of your knowledge
and the candor of elsewhere,
to describe yourself keep nothing
in their suns or in mine!

To the petty song of a revolution
gather the hurdles of your life,
barricades that will somehow
erect a limit to the infinite!

PERDICA

A blade of knowledge
for a young soldier
he was there your survivor
of news flashes.
Let's go old bag, let's taunt
this warm Astrolabe
victimize the stem of a lilac
fires of Lesbos
and the third estate!
Everything is allowed in Sanskrit.
To hatch in troubled water
eggs of light
to deify the earth
at the price of boredom,
it was you who predicted it
the enamel conch
and the rudder
of an old barge leaking time!
The treasure vault
keeps the bounty
but throughout the body
for the same reasons
the good filters the shoddy!
Go ahead despot
convert your plan of attack
into other visions,
from the dark blue flanks
of the Aegan sea
I barely got back myself
believe me.
The dead passion
so strongly altered the laws,
I don't know anymore
if it's him or you!

THE WANDERING BARD

The chasms are communicating
and the nights too.
The suns are magnets
but not for long.
And I at the bottom of the abyss
and you in the sun
we will find each other
there,
towards other nights
the abyss and the sun, my two faces!

Portrait of the void
black gold
bottomless
the scale
of all overlaid blues screeches
nameless

and I run in the whirlwind
leave my body there
call of fluid
and look of death

fear...

Ballet of a shadow towards light
give me your hand!
Nothing more.

A wail in the landscape
endless.

Wooden splinters
in my armor
tints of steel for my trip,
I go back and forth
it's that simple.

No more than yesterday would I take
a child's music box,
toward wherever
and in playful exchanges
I go back and forth
it's that simple.

To muddy the best of the lot
turn the feelings stale
overcome the death knell
and on this plan,
go back and forth
it's that simple.

The candlestand to catch
starlings on a shelf,
to spoil the chorus
in a dignified manner
I go back and forth
it's that simple.

Beware the wicked threshold
and its wild flights,
knowledge burns
be prudent!
Go back and forth
it's that simple.

Burned at the flank
the source groans
a spark
a skiff.
To the thirsty eyes
the cry of joy responds
like the others
the cry of anguish
the layers of fear.
And under the hands
hirsute spring...
May the somber chord sink!
Two strangers saw each other again.
To bank my life
on the illusion
of being one,
and to be mistaken!

To plant my body
on a green canvas
and recall a stranger.
In the cluster of dead glimmers
half naked
I dive into
what no longer wishes to exist!
Turn to the rhythm of my desire
and yours too.
And to portray you
on a backdrop of words,
I deprived
my entire being!

THE WANDERING BARD

I asked
you and others too
but not the shadows
for chance
dressed in numbers
I forged
this stranger
with the hands of a queen
the tears of a blizzard!

Through him
through you
I decoded
this other night with full forms
and an old man's gestures!

Then I gave back the psalmody
a deaf cantor was belting out
beyond the credos of life
he spoke to himself of eternity.

Between his nights
between your cross
I shared
this crazy love
like a sorcerer's larva.

This hard love grafted with lightness
and tangles
but it's to him, to this stranger
the wandering bard that I gave
my parodies and my secrets!

My spring is not the spring of wild fauns.
It arrives alone
in wintertime
without a cortege of birds
or green debauchery!
My spring is a sanctuary
in the bile of the everyday.
My spring is nude
my spring is pure
that is its only flaw.
My spring is a kouros
under the windswept sky of Attica.

You have a taste for my victories
and the modesty of my desires,
despite the glimmers of darkness
and the clarities of memory,
I'm back from the stars
for the scent of spindrift
for a warm awakening
under a childlike sun
for a sea that rolls
and never goes far.
It's for you the damned
that I lived tomorrow!
Do you know the refrain
of dead galaxies
and what I culled from them—
it's you who took it back.
On giant algae
with strong arms
I lowered my sail
and booted the pirates,
buccaneers of space
with tattooed souls
millions of lights
for stars gone astray.
I folded the guardrail
on the old chains,
locked the steerage
and took in my sailboat.
You will not see me again
at the helmsman's seat!

Is it you Melisande
is it you who describes
the eyes of Pelleas
in orbit, at night?

I am a passerby
at the bedside of a goblin,
a voiceless stranger
whom fear sublimates,
a different person
much like the sail
of a tired old boat
that canvasses hearts.
Fire is a mortar
and the walled-in snow
under the assaults of refrains
has poured out boredom.
Put away your sweet nudes
the cry of shunned stars
has been thrust upon my life
sordid and languorous
an expired caress.
I would mow your steps
deform the echoes
and acquit the gambling atoms.
Why did you take a risk on me?

I pretend to harm
not a sound...
You are the watcher
on a leafy island
of stale thoughts.
The swamp is invaded with remnants of light.
A monologue with two players
the heavens could not care less!
It's not in the blessed order
to have understood...and to remain silent!

Then I will return
there where I come from
Asclépiade!
I will return to the great deep
from where every sketch comes back
holding You by the hand
by the body by the voice
with You through the mud
with You through the gesture
and through love absolved!
I will have the courage
all those I betrayed
all those I doubted
we will all go clad in light
and I "will be."
Nothing more to add.
You will take my breath
I want your truth
Asclépiade!
Does the path divert you?
Make your childhood speak
ask it why.

Blessed be the contempt of hands!

My body is a jetty of fear
bosom of the moon,
giving to sleep the time to love
and then its rancor.
Blessed be the contempt of hands,
rotproof!

Soul of my landscape where is your heresy?
Take back your languor.
My teeth have been worn down
towards indifference.

THE PROPHET

You are my madman
your stone's water flows in vain
the sands have eroded the innards of the Sinai
the land is an anvil
for alloyed sounds!
Ardor of an intrusion
you who harvest my triumphs
who are you?
Swarthy are the eyes of the peacock
I'm just an afterthought
coiled against the hollow of your instants!
Your soul is an oblong vice
dotted with lost savors
found again
unfinished
extended
to the sound of water
flowing through the gate.
Why do you come so late?
Horrible lethargy
vast plenitude
elegy
of my quietude!

In what crazed doldrums did you plunder these games?
You sing a lullaby to agony
valet to your pleasures
and to better love us, you offer death,
chaotic worlds
erected into statues,
the breath of a fairy
and spittle of a crane.
Submit to the swaying of a sailboat
close your sandy eyes
reverse the colors to the rhythm of the sea—
I am your champion
keep me in the dance!

The hours are unedited
and I am stillborn.
The reversed tempo
in waves of pine needles
has reconstructed
the child I was!
Yesterday or today
the incongruent genesis
deterred my joy,
cry for this other thing
anguish in the depths of my being,
flow of tinder and ashes
frosted by horror,
an impotence!
There you are
deferred in the nuptials of the other,
I am the Persephone
of toppled worlds.

False like a hailstorm in the heart of summer
false like a sea that fancies itself inspired
false like a destiny trapped in a quagmire
false like the appeal of flesh for rent
false like a pardon extended so tight it stings.
False, false, false
more than a winter sky offering a soft sun
more than dawn in hell
more than saints on their knees
more than your banner
and more than bittersweet fruits!

To name you I start over
no one will see me where I am
listening to the miracle's complaints
seeking you in the darkness to cut
throats with complicit eyes terrified,
distorting the dream at the risk of making it eternal
I drag you along
into the hollow of my frozen thirst.
Arc of a shadow
cut with marble and numbers
where are you going?
To record your flight?
Ghost woman, I look farther ahead
to the course of your gaze
and catching you
I feel your body plummeting!

To be
the infinite tenderness of your indifference
and to love you, color of prey!

THE LITTLE GIRL AND THE GERANIUM

Far... Far...
Towards your blue geranium
a little girl
who prays novenas
on the blue geranium
crushing my dreams!
I implored her to approach...
An earthen jar with a broken collar
I lost my way... So what?
Doubled my flesh
I vanquished the shelter
and our detours!
A little girl
under the blue geranium
who finds sorrow again,
the sorrow of always.
Processions of hunger
my births
hands in supplication
an escape
and the blue geranium
tired of innocence
directed my shadow
to the forgiveness of the living,
on the blue geranium
as blue as a girl's eyes,
gray slate
with yellow strips
enchanted,
to have understood unknowingly
the soul of the geranium
as blue as it is perfect!

Nothing matters to me.
I leaned tenderly
against the leg
of a bird.
Without me the depths of the water
can only be abysses.
The algae wrinkled
faces
and the heart of words
no longer knows your image.
Beneath the water
a gold piece…
that the chimeric currents
exile
to the banks where the sea returns.

I wanted you anxious
yesterday not today
would you know how to detach
a burdensome fantasy?
Why did you distract me
from other important nothings
I was sinking into?
Here my illusions
at your place the almosts
of a distorted tale.
You are this universe
in its unchanged phase!
I don't want an esthete
in the pursuit of my nights.
On impotent masks
I melted regret
specter of notes
cacophony
my pieces of moon
to stun an elf,
then wanting as a prevision
to emasculate life
based on a proverb.

LANDSCAPE

The melodic drizzle
the dunes and the silence
a landscape in three movements of the brush.
I at the resurgence of your cadence
we, on our backs.
To drink to the haze of sandstorms
crawl to the fig tree—
malingering is the inevitable
fate of schoolchildren!

ADOLESCENCE

A fair complexion
the soft green eyes,
my wild hair
strewn in braids
all have a history
a history of contrived love,
without much else
not even memories
to wax nostalgic!
I extol the beauty of girls.
The taunts and jibes hurled at them
are nothing more than garlands and myrtles
to collect!
For Melusine and her cloud
your safeguards,
but the blue countries are ageless
and devoid of turmoil!
Wearing fancy boots
chests out
ah! the showoffs,
epigrams with searching hands
under their smocks.

Yes to the dreams
of a demi-God
with unearthly weapons,
because from Lesbos
to Athena
the games are doubled!

Once again
it's the regret of things,
the eternal one
nothing will be
like it was
today without yesterday
a restless vacation,
to restore our union
through ties of kinship!

Crowned the mountain
moves forward
and rumbles
a pure enthusiasm
infantile
revolting.
Whence the charity
blissful apathy
of a pitiful and
senile flame tree...
You are God my youth
a boastful God
a hidden God
a God of laziness
a hanged God
with an open fist
stunted
already,
what you will become
without being
my melody.

Dalila
dear friend
I will attempt the opposite,
evoke the present
and bring back the night.
Intoxicated by your color
drunk with audacity,
I simply transcribe
the songs you forget!

Hear the eloquence of colors shivering
under the sun of nowhere
the tones of a fervent music
sparkle,
a music to make nuns
twist their hips.
I decided to live
to transgress the taboos
that rhyme with scorn.
Secretly you join me
on the ardent planet
a flooded whim
your muses
pale from boredom flee
always slower
to dampen the wrinkles
the sleeping space
awakening
astonished
to march far
into a sea of fauns
irreversible.
Archangel
carbon stamps
have marked your eras
as unknown
misunderstood
intertwined and vanquished
in the eyes of a return
to you, cut off from images,
the whole world
will gravitate
under our caresses
and the swings of a pendulum!

Your hands
my abandonments
a bunker
a booth
toward the madness of nameless eyes!

The pillars of failure
have erected this myth.
Vanquished my child-god,
that is what we are,
destined to give
to the verbiage of men
the secrets of the gryphon
and those of the unicorn,
rejected…
And yet
the diligent student
has translated our clashes
into carafes of bottled sky.
Keep your wine
I only have left to offer
noxious incense
of rituals and vampires!

Man with slim waist
imposter in need of mud
I knelt toward
rotten ideas
impervious to remorse
where your harvesters bathe,
admire a body sawed off...

The flower is born and reborn
until it perfects its quality.
At that moment, it disappears!

In hell's dialect
I preached the unthinkable,
it's here
not elsewhere
that the truth gives up!

I bet my stars on
these night games.
They're serving drinks
at the fairies' Lent
by the big oak tree
in the marshland
where the fireflies congregate
under your devoured steps.
The panicked woodlands
vomit the cities' air
and my rivulets carry
the black of all eyes.
Cry peasants
sit enthroned
there are no more bards
no sap clinging
to the currents of winds.

Wandering
my furtive
dash
predicted
in the driftings of the redemptive gesture.
Here is the death knell that sounds
a sudden knell.
Vertigoes of flowers
with banns of equinoxes
have a different rhythm
a dead warmth.
Wandering
her furtive
dash
predicted
in the driftings
tethered to your fear.

A trough of sandalwoods
to drink to your loves,
an attic of pleasures
to elude my scorn,
and you in the body's depth
you who presents
the songs of Jezebel
to the prestige of brambles,
become color
quirky time
metallic wind
a laughingstock
with a leprous neck,
the magic
of a newborn!

You my youth
bathed in laughter
mandarin eyes
unique,
here are the bodies
where I look for myself
without finding
the intensity
of magical fears!

THE AGE OF EMBERS

The little girl is a bougainvillea
she lingers in the gardens in her scarlet dress
the archimandrite here is unsightly
he has imaginary legs
he hides in his blanket of travels
the fire the bread the honey and the latent sand
he's more than twenty years old their god
he loves our anguish and feels at home there
the little girl is a bougainvillea
from the country where birds sing hymns
pronounced like the archway of a monastery made of copper
the little girl has a new smile
she releases her bees in the deserted port
and sees nothing of nights
because she is afraid of them

Then you rose from the depths of the ocean
when the sea was vertical
there is no thunderstorm
only the sound of frightened birds
gone where the thorns have merged with night
I am each fold of earth always renewed
because the sea is a ringdove
there is no trail
only the cry of forms found again

Hands heavy with rain
the metallic race shames the smooth waves
fresh water that passing stars pollute.
Walled-in sleep
the dungeons of childhood open a dark garden
to the sky of the high seas
are you this stranger who lowered to earth
places a necklace of stones around the fold of the tides?
Are you what turns into the lover and the awakening
the blaze of a bird at the outskirts of the sun?
At last I know the naked pulse of summer
the one that bats eyes and seeks.

Like these decrepit walls
that every night attempt to erect gardens on the dunes
like a sky that moves on farther still
under the lash of the day's whip
a cluster of masts where the ports get entwined
you know nothing more about me than a combustion of colors
like sleep hoisted by a pulley
when the earth moves and splinters
like a tree nourished by honey and war
I am the wind that abates
when the bird is no more.

There are paths of ashes where the flowers end
and the gildings of Byzantine virgins pass...
It's the young mountain where the blaze marches on
where under the rocks like a forgotten temple
the other side of your sun sleeps...
Their granite pitchers at times turn water into wind
and the flocks of birds rise towards Orion sculpted by earth
there are paths more weary still
when the ringdoves depart...

Others say nights are deserts and victories
and knives sharpened by thirst
and animals tortured in their eyes
in the cries that are let out
others say nights inflate citadels
if this age is alive under the marine rock
nights do not battle
nights do not struggle
others say nights are wings of Gomorrha
and narrow caravels around the reefs
that children invent to tether the sea
under the fading withering waves
the night that hears what it touches
never struggles again

There are coastlines where the waves are musicians
where the sea is a garden
where the winds are so many pyres burning
there are ramparts around you
and moats as deep as a drowned man
there are unreal flowers more beautiful standing against the earth
and liquid prayers time has frozen in royal crimson
there are eyes in each stone
and the grand anguish of mornings.
O darkness that burns the forests of an indulgent winter
remember that the wind of battles
carries the stench of steel and bodies
higher into the clouds.
Would you notice in an open hand
traces of a child following the roses?
Battles create a thicker night
than a swarm of ravens overhead.
O darkness burning the birds of a humid land
remember that these mountains have hidden powers
in the folds of their ancient layers
and that the water wounded by the islands
places a fountain in the sun.

Bring you back to whom?
But I am no longer there I have changed my name
my eyes have the color of absence
yesterday is nothing other than a window that rattles
and before me a basin of holy water—
bring you back to whom?
God is indifference
he is there simply when the fields are in bloom
when beaches bridle at the scorn of wind
but he derives no pleasure from it
after the nothingness of words there is the nothingness of gestures
and the moons carry on
God does not hold them back.

To follow the water because it's red and naked
dressed in the marine sun that slices
the roots of fear splattered at night
the sun has a hard time being a ball of fire
a sea that snorts
the whorl deified by waters that neigh
when the hoofs of war trample on their eyes
to follow the bird the clouds offer
familiar like grass cruel like an instant
the bird full of fleeting universes
unbridled
the bird torrent of seas

Would you come back if I said the earth is at your fingertips
like a branch scorched but already cooled?
The birds died several times brushing against your blond hair
they had adopted the sea as a vice
because of the sonorous algae
and paths that unwind
slowly
too late for each instant to be born
kneeling before faces the color of the Eucharist
like throats taken from cattle devouring a ray of sun
would you come back if I said the sea is at your fingertips?

The sun and steel coffers of naked trees
hatred breathed into the stone
you are a crushed plant
the lair of the man not yet born
in seasons hatched by the sea
Africa
your stars are flowers of sand
the luster of your thighs will carry the wind where silence digs
the rains have snuffed out their voices
they caress the throat
Africa
and the art of hanged birds
dies until tomorrow

Tomorrow will be the hermits
and these wise men the wind carried from column to column
tomorrow will be corals disowned by the sea
they announce rain and the ark
the faun that unleashes the same indifference
towards man accused of having taken from the land
ruins we would like muted
tomorrow will be the prey

Over there a beach without fences returns
and your night bracelets tally the remains of a worn-out sun
it has lived this sky
and the sea birds have decided to laugh about it
because cannons have wind-like gestures
they are women your wars all the way to the dead grass
in the ashes of god holding a pen
in the body of lovers this morning
because noontime suns have undressed the sea
in the country where the leaves
fall like tears

The blues are only shrieks
the yellows curves
and time emerald because I want it so
to caress a body
narrow like all that is beautiful
slow
to make these full-blown hatreds last
hatreds more precious than love
fire is this mirage swallowed by your eyes
and the stone a solid barge
puts a fractured god that does not recognize
the sun-mills where the sea is a legend

He offered his waves to basalt doors
waves deep bodies that last an eternity in the sand
the folds of the sea are breathless birds
they bring icefields floating under the boats of men
like aged beasts with faces slashed by divine justice
he cracked the hardened water
and these mages of wind that each spindrift clings to
when Saturn having escaped from the arms of the orante
becomes a boat of rowers the horizon drags along

In Nizhny Novgorod the sea is forgotten
in the eyes of the fisherman
who softly picks up the shadow of the fig-tree under the wind
he places transparencies in ruins
the sonorous bells ring
in Nizhny Novgorod where the sun hears and amplifies prayers
pyres of faces peer at the cold sky
all fired up with birds

I am an ending to a prayer
a sky that will change its armor to a portal
the mist feels cold only during that month
when you arrive warm
to taunt the birds who are there painted on the field
I am the sand that sheds layers and discovers sand
where birds are masters
where colorless peoples have invaded the sea
where arms end in rings one can only escape
because the sky is yours
a wet god emerges

It's the peddler of chimeras
they hang at the tip of a spider web
for a long time for as long as it might take him to forget
these vast plains where the land
tells of birds adorned with sheets of rain
and who could unpack the night and trace bridges of light
the birds opened themselves
to swallow cities in all corners of the world
then spit them back on the plains
like the aftermath of typhoons how the sea
regurgitates fish in abundance
the cities at the four corners of the sky have draped all their
mornings with shadows
there are trees around each shadow to protect it
and a stream sheds its colors to water it
it's the peddler of chimeras
who has forgotten at the tip of a spider web
the birds who savor the earth

What are islands good for?
Tayo loved only me
besides that was why Tayo went away
toward a sun so close a flick of the tongue could wet it
Tayo loved only me and then the seashells
those that have no ears and those that know
but Tayo left with what he found
come closer there is water to drape your body
I'll take you by the eyes
my arms are seasons and a vigil for the storm
Tayo loved only me and the birds
that are the couriers of time
come closer my lips are slitting the salted earth
it's only hardened water
one's loins adjusting to the great departure
Tayo loved only me and I became the country
come back Tayo to the heart of the message
the sea is a cathedral and its waves are bell towers
the moons have taken me away and shattered me
each day of this era between your teeth Tayo.

I see you as embers and cage
as in Rome one sees the stones
on a morning riddled with night's remnants
rising in the sap of laureled balconies
I see you as flesh and cage
like a snake made of bricks
scrubbing the sun against its green backbone
in Rome
where sleep is a field of relics

She is dead this sea suffocated by treasures
the shipwrecked have crawled
under the complacent eyes of those forever drowned—
who speaks of fauns?
You who are alive target your hatred
scratch the liquid days
dead is the sound of flowers
it leaps the summer months
and with a stroke of redness stifles a wet winter
the one found in the eyes of the drowned.

I believe in you because warm
like a forgotten lake
like an open field under threat of ravens
like an ageless country
the sky extended its tongue of fog
and launched the universe
initiated by chance

Where the door's hinges rattle and shake
what doesn't yet have a name
is the wind crucified between all our words
he says I am the wind standing
even if the liquid arms of birds in union
turn their inertia into a lifeline
I know where the road veers
but it does not exist

Embers have wrapped this crown of thorns
I saw my blood born and you disappeared
no message spoiled the forest
it's woven not to see
the thyme believes the snails that listen
at the soil's edge
but they don't have ears
and so
the gesture has for long undone a snail
a dreamer
and a mage
who shatter the opaque forest
a resplendent sun and useless time.
Vania, talk
talk
say
Vania, forget
the thyme will never know
neither will I at the end of the dance
besides a fishbowl is pretty small.

Frescoes have librettists
words have regrets: to be with your fellow creatures
thirst is quenched by the night of the dying
and the maps of time change buccaneers
that is how the rose will give birth to salt
a garden where wells cleave to the earth
my tears rediscovered will unleash the waters.

This is where I am god
where the ponds brood over steely storms
and tears are better seen in the summer
your naked fingers make an hourglass
and my body molding a mask
gives back to the survivor the taste of high seas
this is where I am flesh

Tomorrow returns from elsewhere
weighing as much as audacity
banished from all songs
it's you who replaces it
woman with gestures
grasped by the wind's scars

You never knew the rip currents
cages of petrified algae
that see a carnal accord break against the rocks
there is no more hell there is no more wind
at the duels the games are fixed—
matador who are you laughing at?
You never knew the lances one extends to better puncture eyes
the amber necklace of hands and the well of confessions
oracles fall silent in the presence of a god.

Once upon an evening
the sea was listening on its knees
to the corals calling the storms at the belfry
and their rapacious tints
turned into laughter at the mouth of the naked atoll
a pointed evening
with waves lapping the reefs
with winds drawing
starry morsels of gigantic shipwrecks

I think a pile of leaves
then a body laid out
melted on the ground
with leaves on top
I think a pile of leaves and hair too
and peats of honey
the knell has nothing to do with the unbridled storm
a midnight sun at the heart of your gaze
where leaves cover a slice of sky

The seated worshippers at the heart of the mirage
transported immobile the unbearable fusion
to the grazing field
defunct like a life the jasmine eyes blinked their names
the necropolis sheltered gazes
perhaps the hawk will wear out its beak on our flesh
or will he do like others?
I am your fear tied to fate
I create the emptiness in everyone.
Vast incongruity of parallel beings.

The columns of seas and castles of mud
keep hell in the jet-black sky
you are earth
like a bouquet of salt carried by a fairy
you are earth
only greens have hope
they embody the tone of the universe
and the friendship of moons that know perhaps
you are earth splintering into another matrix
towards a latent world

A bouquet of birds encircle a fountain
it was during other nights
a pearl clings to the bars of a nest
and carried by the wind my dreams are harnessed
to the clocks' ticking
fire bites its fingers
hurry a magician to translate
it's a dance with oboes
and in the palace the cats glow!
Three stairways with cracked voices
black is worn for this occasion
and the coffers have the soul of a cornflower
where dolls are cultivated
and the erasures of old notebooks
disguise themselves in the gypsy tarot
the dead birds will tell why.

At my place
there are gardens where the desert haunts
where on the sonorous womb of royal galleys
chained to sleep a moon ends
a grail of nomads they think vast
cannons followed by clouds!
At my place
there are birds full of trees
with poison kindness
summer precedes spring
and demurely
a branch performs miracles.

Listen
it's never the forest that unrolls
a raging ocean around the hawks
the forest sees boredom and anoints you spring
the star that rises is
for her or for me
chased away by the wind

Robed in hatred
transparent
famished
eyes like a vulture's carve up memory
into colored pieces

For what she represents
and not for what she is
for sequins of stars
tapered in the shape of regrets
to fix the coquetry of a smile
to cut away the apparition
of your ribboned pack of hounds

I live with lucid memories that flee an uncertain summer
bursting like these fires we speak of that are quickly extinguished
I sleep in shattered memories
laying on the knees of a child
who will never feel the joys of a playground
because he is too dead
and the wolves and hollow owls will enact miracles
and the four leaf clover will say I grow
under the steps of those who are not ashamed to believe
the others will forget

The night that breathes
has shrunk your shadow
under the portico of a wooden sky
this night that forges ahead
like a devout looter
and the familiar crocuses
have worn out
the night that lodges
at the bottom of each error
a world to be deployed

I see eyes perfect like autumn
acidic
summer's forests come here to discover
the capsizing of boats sailing towards fear
a day unlike the one you know
a day where the tides have brass nostrils
shoeless planters to better discover God
borrowed from autumn the art of moving colors
they went a long way against the big-sky
and under the mountain where water crosses the field
ivory and sleep extend the harvests
the night you mature on the plains of autumn
joins under the mountain the horizon's embers
acidic
like these eyes that resemble autumn

Your colors have bled happily
a bed of mad desires
fuzzy like a dream
that jettisons its return
and joins the movements
of night's precipices

I love you most in the sanctuary
and the doors are closing
old jewel box
to better discover you
a chalice in hand
on your knees you are simply
not brown earth
you are not the messenger of invented nights
a stamp of sun on the wilted flowers
old jewel box
I know how to belong to you

There are no more magical fears
your life is here
a thicket of warmth
a handle detached from disquiet
a place where the sky is never what it seems
the greens are renewing themselves
the calm despair
and my other smile
do not recognize you

This museum has charming alcoves
it tells pleasant stories
a sweet summer
the winter insidious and wise
messages destined for no one
why then would we unfurl images
ransack hell's kitchen
and invent kings?

The desert walls stretching into a blue that talks
and the bedrock withering by the sun's spade
tuck your nostalgias under the sea
camel drivers who plant sand and rocks
to better find the lakes where god travels
chisel births in a braid of green sand
and the eyes of the dying
will see in it only dust

Centaur, you are at home at the edge of glass wires
listen, listen to the heart of seasons breathe
while digging the earth we make doors tremble
quilts shake
and summers ripen...
Centaur, of course over there
under the music of violins
you are a conductor of worlds!

Polar ships
you will make the waters flow
towards a sun that resides in memories
when the sky loads its slingshot
the cobblestones assail the darkness that retracts

Polar ships
under the Milky Way
a horde of stars
ready to renew
the giant scarabs at the end of light-years

Awakened the hips unleashed the music
adorned the mirage of rains with regalia
knotted under a ring the song's remnants
and froze the firewood with tears of poison ivy

an age when birds could lasso the sun!

You have the green of mourning born in galaxies
a comet-like jewel offers a chronicle
to the future of others
one can count on him
disguised as a puppet my special key opens
for him the floodgates of boredom!

Enough troubadours have sung for flowers
played the broken song of stars
and sewn the ruffles of waves
dressed like elders
he does not wait
it's towards tomorrow that he goes blushing with certainty
and the lost lotus on the outskirts of the island
traces a haunted joy

Some are ornate like an English garden
others undressed like Arabia
the most beautiful however
cannot be compared to earth
except perhaps if man created god

Water that flows living is bereft of laughter
the lakebed craves the sun
escaping the crystal galleys
at the foot of a tabernacle a city
that moves that moves

Christ
is the other I await him
he has eyes of glass
the beak of a red raven and quite a past
a hieratic sorrow makes his cobblestones shine
he says yesterday sun
you were born of a mirage
that is not where I found you
breaths have expanded
a cascade is draped with the remnants of the escape
....
Madonna Madonna
he is never resuscitated!